To Madge —

Here's something different
for you to use with your
flower-arranging skill and your
garden's lovely Hawaiian blossoms!
We think of you + R.V. often —

with love,

Ruth + Silver

September

D1475185

IKEBANA

by Senei Ikenobô

translated by
Kaichi Minobe

HOIKUSHA

PREFACE

Resisting wind and rain, a tiny flowering plant keeps breathing dreaming its bright future. Its serious activity to live is powerful enough to move people. The fundamental aims of the flower arrangement that stand above the shape, the color and the beauty of formation, are to express men's sympathy towards the tiny life of plant and their expectation for its future. Ikebana is created being based upon the noble and spiritual interchange between men and flowers.

The form of Ikebana speaks for the flowers that endeavor to adapt themselves to their surroundings.

Here lies the key that reveals the secret of Japanese Ikebana which sometimes appears mysterious.

Senei Ikenobô
The Forty-fifth
Head master of
Ikenobô School

CONTENTS

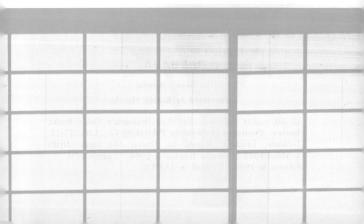

Daily Life Ikebana

Our Living and Ikebana

Against almost all arts which are to be seen and to be appreciated, Ikebana is lined up with the art of creating. A quite few people are enjoying the delight of creating by arranging flowers. In Ikebana, unlike Chanoyu or tea ceremony, the composition is born as a result of acting. The composition also provides the home with ornamental utility. Furthermore, the fascination of the art (Ikebana) lies in the beauty of the flowers and plants used as materials.

Flowers are beautiful both in old times and in the present time. The colour of flowers gives our mind a comfortable tone. Even children enjoy looking at flowers. Tenshin Okakura, famous artist, wrote about flowers in his book, "The Book of Tea".

In joy or sadness, flowers are our constant friends. We eat, drink, sing, dance, and flirt with them. We wed and christen with flowers. — How could we live without them? It frightens one to conceive of a world bereft of their presence. What solace do they not bring to the bedside of the sick, what light of bliss to the darkness of weary spirits? Their serene tenderness restores to us our waning confidence in the universe even as the intent gaze of a beautiful child recalls our lost hopes. When we are laid low in the dust it is they who linger in sorrow over our graves.

It is man's natural action to arrange flowers when a man turns his eyes to flowers and he is impressed with them. People do it for the joy of creating. Thus, Ikebana has been blended into people's daily life.

Ikebana is not for a few specialists. Also it is not limited to only special circumstances. Not only in a living room but in an office or a hall it can be arranged for decoration. Even in a bus, Ikebana, seems to be a most suitable ornament. Then, Ikebana is not only beautiful to look at but also inspiring.

The inspiring element is the very one which our predecessors fervently sought after in Ikebana. Tenshin's saying, "restores to us out waning confidence in the universe" does not aim at prettiness of flower, but at the vitality and the movement of mind resonant with life. There we feel a joy in arranging flowers, and then we find the clue which leads us to Ikeru, or to arrange, from to Sasu, or to stick. The most important significance of Ikebana is in the blending into daily life and in EXISTING JUST NOW.

2. Nageire
   Dahlia · Decolourized fern/Green thin top vase

The room takes on life with Ikebana. The Japanese home is especially suited to Ikebana because of its manner of construction. When the action of Ikebana is brought into the quietness of a room is filled with charm.

4

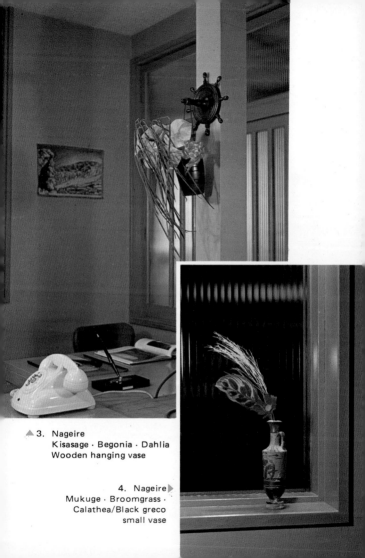

▲ 3. Nageire
Kisasage · Begonia · Dahlia
Wooden hanging vase

4. Nageire ▶
Mukuge · Broomgrass ·
Calathea/Black greco
small vase

Scene ornamented by Ikebana — leisure time

The Mind to Arrange Flowers

Being more beautiful than twinkling stars in the space, a stream of water on the ground, blue of the broad sea and shining jewels, a flower may catch a human mind. The clear beauty of flowering plants leads us to a sweet recollection. The softness of trembling flowers in the faint wind and the brightness of vivid flowers under the sunshine seem to say something to us.

The various shapes changing in accordance with the four seasons reveal the continuous growing of the unmovable form which may be called fate. Flowering plants having their own charactor extend their branches, open their leaves and make their blooms to the light. There is a kind of order, and we will find the will of nature which breathes slowly in the air and grows ceaselessly in accordance with an order. Thus, the flowering plants which create a moving harmony, moment by moment, through living, do not fail to impregnate our mind with new impressions continuously. You find beauty out of flowers not through logic but through intuition, nevertheless the intuition is supported by the sympathy with the will of flower. People touch with the mind of plants, and they find their desire on the flowering plant. In our mind to arrange flowers we do desire to clarify our inspiration as a form. The inspiration grows when we touch the flower's mind much more than through the beauty of shape and colour; then, we know our own mind.

On the impulse to arrange flowers we try to put them in a vase or in a bottle. However, the flower in a container does not show the vivid beauty as it did on field or mountain. The beauty of the flower is just the same; nevertheless, the flower loses the taste which it possessed when it grew in nature extending its branches at ease and breathing comfortably in the air. When flowers are picked they are taken from the order secretly hidden in nature. The purpose of arranging flowers is to give cut and broken branches the order that they had in nature. Furthermore it is to create utmost natural beauty which shows the motivity of life, through creating the variation adapted to the supposed surrounding.

5. Nageire
Kinmei bamboo · White
flower camellia/Italian
glass

6. Moribana (Hanging flower)
   Sunflower · Summer wax-tree · Miscanthus/Glass pot

The flower hanging from a ceiling seem to breathe, then the hall has meaty space.

7. Nageire
   Dahlia · Arocasia · Oriental bittersweet/Italian pottery

   *On the corner of wall, the balance of life begins is kept and
   living space is created.*

9

Structure of Ikebana

What we want to express in Ikebana is the growth process of floral plants and their earnest activity to reach an ideal. We are impressed by the various beauties of floral plants which try to live on in various natural surroundings, and then we try to move them to container as they are. However we cannot move the floral plant which is growing in nature into container as it is. Even if we move a piece of branch as it is, we cannot always retain the beauty which the floral plant showed in its natural scene. In order to retain it we need to establish several settings.

A traditional Ikebana is arranged in an upright shape at the just location on the tokonoma.

Usually aesthetic form needs to accompany stability. In general, it is the form which has balance in itself. A long body aflains stability when it lies. Living floral plants, however, have the energy to stand up; they become unstable when they are laid down. The energy to make stability from top to bottom is always acting to them. So far as we try to show the growing energy of plants in Ikebana, we have to have a hypothesis that the energy is still acting in plants after they become Ikebana. When the hypothesis is kept securely in mind, floral plants just become Ikebana. The floral plant used as material is not to be put in a vase, but it is to have its own form to stretch up from the vase as a starting point and to stand up with spring.

A living thing changes continually. This change is produced by the continual balance of power between the will to grow and the surroundings which feed plants, which is called, the grace of Heaven and Earth, such as rain, dew, wind, and snow. Through the distortion and the degree of change which are made of the conflict between these two powers, Ikebana suggests the surrounding of plants, produces an atmosphere, and reflects the desire of the arranger. The floral plant stretching up from a starting point, a vase, shows the effect of the earth on the lower branch, reflects that of the air on the stretching branch, and expresses the will of plant itself on the twig. When it comes to be formalized, they become, what is called, Ikebana's THREE MAIN BRANCHES, such as Shin, Soe and Tai.

8. 'Rikka   Acacia · Dahlia · Oriental bittersweet ·
             Torch lily · Windmillpalm bamboo/Square
             vessel with ears and legs

Traditional Rikka which is the most classical form, could be the ornament of modern wall by changing treatment of materials.

Ikebana is very versatile. For example, Shoka which is rooted in ancient history, is in conformity with todays life. The bright figure of the torch-lily and dahlia stretching up, shows us modern brightness in a classical atmosphere.

9. Shoka
   Torch lily · Dahlia/Pottery with violin type top

Materials and Ikebana

To arrange flowers is to cut the parts of plants and to reorganize them as a new shape. However each floral plant, even if we cut the branch and take off the leaf, still tells us its background in which it grew. It may be said that each material has its own will. From this view-point the material of Ikebana is fundamentally different from paints and plaster. This special condition has an important influence on the composition of Ikebana.

When I see children's group marching with various dresses, I recall the special condition of Ikebana. Children act after their teacher's conduct, while each act in one's own way intermittently. The form of children marching with the hopeful faces to an unknown world is joyful and pretty to see. Each shows his own inherent wild nature, while each blends into the group.

One of the objects of arranging flowers is to produce a unity of wills, through encouraging the branch's and leaf's own will. Floral plants take on life — life with future as they are arranged so as to retain more natural settings and forms. Only then, Ikebana brings inspiration to men's mind as a living and acting body.

Naturally growing
old-world arrowhead

However, the soul of floral plants is reflected not only on the posture but on the colour, the quality and the form of small parts. All parts of a floral plant is filled with the inherent beauty of plants. From this view-point, there comes the second purpose of arranging flowers.

If we abandon the posture of plants and compose the various parts, heterogeneous parts become irritative, resistive and resonant by arranging them in a row. Sometimes the parts glitter harmoniously as stars in the heaven. The sharpness and the powerfulness of plants seem to be today's breath. Such an Ikebana is, what is called, "Mental Ikebana".

Postural Ikebana is important as the living Ikebana by which we get hospitality and purity through devoting ourselves to floral plants. While Mental Ikebana is going to be a new living Ikebana as a positive Ikebana which enables us to recognize the existence of our present lives bearing mutation on our backs throughout life.

Mysteriously pretty looking monstera

Style of Ikebana

Ikebana has inherited a long tradition with the background of daily life. Then it has given birth of various styles in accordance with each era.

Of those styles Rikka and Shoka survived while Nageire and Moribana are flourishing as modern styles. Moreover new styles adapted to today's living will be born.

11. Nageire
    Kerria/Cobalt bent jar

10. Moribana
    Black-pine · Setaria-Italica · Cockscomb/Broad top
    porcelain with shell's crests

Nageire flower in 1688 — 1703

Nageire and Moribana

Nageire was named from the shape which it takes; it looks as if one threw branches of flowers into a vase. If we put the side branch along the top of the vase, the flower becomes stabilized and then it becomes Nageire flower.

Moribana was named from the technique by which we put the flower over a vase as if heaping them up.

Though it looks easy to arrange, both Nageire and Moribana require difficult techniques.

When we put a floral plant into a deep vase, the branch of the flower is supported by the top of the vase and is stabilized by itself. This is the simple form of sticking flowers. The original form of Nageire started from the sticking flowers. The fundamental requirement of Ikebana, however, lies upon reflecting the scene of natural plants, because its materials are floral plants. Usually natural plants have a main stem and divided branches, and they extend leaves and open flowers. In other words, it is the shape of growing up from the earth.

However, Nageire tries to emphasize a portion of the beauty of branches and leaves. In other wards, partial emphasis has been growing in connection with the simple form of sticking flowers.

Moribana which is a form of sticking flowers in SUIBAN or broad top vase was given birth, but in this case, arrangers intended not to treat a piece of floral plant, but to express the scenery of gregarious plants. Arrangers intended mainly to express the Europeans' colorful beauty. Both Nageire and Moribana have in their background the dominant thought of the then contemporary artists.

While today's Nageire and Moribana both have the aforementioned background, they have changed both in technique and in content. The reason is that they have had to fulfil various requirements of Ikebana as Nageire and Moribana popular instead of retaining traditional forms.

Consequently, Nageire and Moribana get rid of the pursuit of simple scenic expression or colorful beauty. Therefore, they began to create free space by plant's own requirements; the characteristic form coming from its name went out and their forms were transformed into standing style or bowing one. The Nageire and Moribana fused into one form.

12. Moribana
   Calla · Allium/Broad top vase

Looking at the top of a vase from oblique above — The material is stuck in KENZAN, or metalplate with many needles, and it is composed as to express strong appeal by bending to this side.

13 Shoka

Pinetree · Cameria /
Copper bottle with ears

14 Shoka
Young pinetree · Rose /
Bow's feather-shaped porcelain painting iron powder

Shoka

Shoka continues to be loved by many people, because of its uprightness, elegance and dignity.

Nageire and Moribana express a portion of the beauty of plants, while Shoka intends to express the beauty of one or two stumps and the action for living which we find from the posture corresponding with the circumstance.

Cutting flowers in a flower shop, is sometimes called SEIKA (Chinese letters are the same as SHOKA) but it means vivid and fresh flowers. Meanwhile, SHOKA in Ikebana means not only fresh but organic sticking flowers. The expressions, to die or to live, are common to all forms of Ikebana, but they carry the most meaning in Shoka. The reason for this is that those expressions are related to the fundamental structure of Shoka.

Shoka is constructed on an assumption just as Kabuki play is. To express the mysterious vitality of plants is Shoka; the vitality means changing shape following to the plant's own charactor movability and are exposed to light and obstacles between

The key of making Shoka's beauty is found out of the tightness just above the water. The tail of the stem is fixed on a vase, and the stem is stretched up as in a line. Materials are stuck from front to back, play three roles in accordance with the degree of distortion.

Heaven and Earth. Containers are equivalent to the earth and ponds.

The space is supposed to have four corners and lightness and darkness. We presume rain, dew, wind and snow from the distortion of the branch, and plant's own vitality from a twig. Shoka's semilunar type is constructed with the expectation that the lunar will be filled soon.

In the concrete, the material plant is shown standing up from the earth; the main stem stretches from the container; the branches show distortion affected by air in the midst of stretching; the twigs show the strength of vitality to stretch in enduring every obstacle. These distortion and the degree of change suggest the circumstance of the plant, make a mood, and express the enthusiasm of the arranger to the plant's vitality.

Rikka is expected to make reappearance of the beauty and the scenic taste of natural plants over a flower container; those plants are flourishing with harmony or with competition on the top of a high mountain or in a vast field. Rikka's magnificent scale and colourful beauty are made of systematic harmony and repulsion among nine main branches each of which plays a part.

Many plants and trees pile from front to rear, stretching right and left in complicated manner. Though each part of composition seems unnatural, the whole composition makes a mysterious harmony and reflects of the beauty of the scenic natural world.

There we feel the wind blowing in the field and listen to the pulsation of life sounding in the sun beam.

15. Rikka

24

Pinetree · Flowering quince · Iris · Spiraea-thunbergii · Camellia ·
Trumpet-daffodil · Asparagus-lucidus · Freesia · Milliocratus ·
Cornus-officinalis · Loquat/Black painting, hoof shaped jar

25

Rikka

Today we call Ikebana-arrangement IKERU, or arranging in general, however Rikka is called TATERU, or putting up, Shoka is Ikeru, or planting, and earlier Nageire-Moribana is SASU, or sticking in origin. These classifications show an important difference of content, though it seems a simple distinction.

The reason why Rikka is called TATERU originates in decorating Buddha or Shinto's God with flowers. In arranging the flowers, we give the meaning that we establish Paradise. While, in forming the arrangement we realize the common charactor of plants to stretch up.

Rikka does not always take the form like Shoka which we put a floral plant straight in a vase. Even if the branches look natural the truth is that we connect plants with neels and wires according to an object.

Rikka has a much more complicated assumption than Shoka. Its shape is larger and it needs many materials. Each material gives us a suggestion to remind the former natural scene of the material. It is composed to express the circumstances of the natural environment. Then we intend to unite the variations through the internal sympathy of various materials. The fundamental technique of the composition is to give roles to nine main branches, in order to attach them coordination and repulsion, and furthermore to intervals, make so as to give

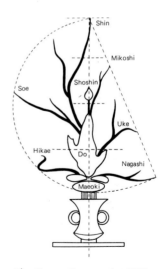

The figure of composing Rikka

them a vivid elasticity.

Nine main branches are named Shin or the most important branch, Soe or the branch next to the central one, Uke or the branch placed at the top or under Shin, Nagashi or the branch at the bottom and stretching sidelong, Hikae or one at the bottom and stretched obliquely backward, Mikoshi or those at the top stretching out of the center, Shoshin or that of central view-point, Doh or important lines placed at the center, and Maeoki or one in the forefront.

In a vase, we put a needle plate. We fasten a leg to the tail of the main branch or the accessory's branch, and then we sharpen the leg to stick into needle plate. To the branches, we attach small branches and leaves as they are natural. Therefore we use scissors and several tools.

27

16. Phantom light
Allium · Coral/Modified pottery
with two mouthes and two legs

17. Remembrance ▶
Antherium · Sunflower · Hamamelis/
A pair of vase painted floral plants,
each with a ear

Attempt to Create New Form

The attempt to create a new form started in breaking Ikebana's usage. Departing from IKERU or setting, our interest shifts to creating by taking notice of the stimulus from plant's shape and colour. Ikebana is no longer a living plant, but it appeals us to be an object in space. Then it is going to be created in accordance with a picture in the arranger's mind.

The Bridge to Daily Life

When we see a child digging a hole and playing with clay we smile. The mind of a child is filled with rejoicing in creating a form. We may say that this mind has built the human history, moment by moment. Though we pursue an economic value in life, it is in admiring beauty and in creating things that we enrich the ground of our mind. Ikebana has contributed as much to human life as painting or composing poems. As true as all arts, Ikebana becomes untouchable for common people in proportion as the level of the form and the content rises. Originally Ikebana was intended to express arranger's mind, but it becomes hard for people to feel enthusiasm for creating, because of the pressure of rules.

Today's Ikebana restores freedom through getting out of traditional category, and now has entered into all lives. It has its own place even in an apartment room and at a corner of modern kitchen as well as in a gorgeous hall. Ikebana restored the originality of daily-life Ikebana through uniting with the modern human mind. Then it took various formations according to circumstances. Just as children receive joy in their creation of a certain form or pattern, joyce results in a flower-arranger's mind as they arrange the floral plants in such a way that the feelings of relief and mobility are created with the arrangement. The joyful arrangement is blended into a modern living room with modern human sense. Furthermore, we add new variations, flowing out of modern circumstances, to classic Rikka and Shoka as they leave their traditional rules behind them.

In consequence, Ikebana must be always formed from the arranger's own will. It must result in one's own enjoyment. It must not be a difficult composition for the sake of hardship. When the flexible mind is reflected in the arrangement, a room is filled with brightness and Ikebana gives us hope for tomorrow and enjoyment. Daily-life Ikebana needs not be called "art". If we have a clear mind, we will not fail to create a pretty form.

Mobile by floral plants

19. Rikka
Miscanthus · Gentain · Toad-lily · Gum leaves · Dahlia ·
Small-chrysanthemum · Fringed-iris/Green pottery
with three legs

Bright and relaxed Shoka, and light and simple Rikka; these
two are a new born style in modern life. To the full bloomed
torch-azalea we add the pure and light arc of spiraea; then the
contrast between red and white is splendid. A composition
of Rikka which ignores the traditional rules is as refreshing to
see as an early autumn wind over a field.

20. Shoka
    Torch-azalea · Willow/Broad top vase with horizontal
    stripes

33

21. Shoka
   Lily and Rose/Triangular vase

The Ikebana filled with youthfulness and brightness harmonizes well with Europian shelfs.

Circumstance and Ikebana

Ikebana has restored modern sense through free formation. From the view-point of utility value, Ikebana is managed to become a part of modern life, especially in the home, because of its originality. Home and living equipment are going to change in style. Public institutions, amusement centers and factories are adopting new styles of architecture, and in planning collective residences we are going to adopt new house styles. However old houses still have TOKONOMA, or an alcove which was built for flower arrangements. Ikebana is influenced by the structure and form of houses. Therefore, a new style Ikebana does not always shed luster to the home. Sometimes it is even unfit. Then

Through making a composition, Rikka assimilates with new circumstance.

we have to make a choice between homelike Ikebana and modern Ikebana.

From the view-point of the present housing condition, home is not enough to play a role of modern life, though it is the place to live. Now it is time to reconsider residence as well as Ikebana from outside of tradition and custom. Ikebana has to get out of TOKONOMA and to be placed everywhere in our life as it plays a role of living. When we find the functional space out of our home by ourselves, modern type Ikebana as well as old Rikka or Shoka can be daily life Ikebana with a new mode. Daily-life Ikebana is arranged everywhere in the home by controlling scale, construction and colour.

Ikebana in Spring

Early spring flowers are unsophisticated and fresh-looking while late spring flowers are fascinating. Plants are indeed sensitive to seasons. When I find unexpected green beneath dry grass, I feel spring coming. Such a deep impression to the life of plants becomes an important motive to arrange flowers. It is important for spring Ikebana that its composition contains the arranger's poetical mind and it carries the full mood of spring and the newness as a forerunner of the season.

22   Nageire
Star Lily · Common Gypsophila/Cobalt Guitar-shaped Pot

23 Shoka

Tulip/Wine glass type vase

Spring floral plants grow healthy in favor of warm sunshine without wind and snow. We are impressed by their simplicity and freshness indicating that spring is filled with hope. In bright colour there is a floating dream, and it is sometimes a concealed weakness indicating the absence of hardship.

Such a spring mood is shown by the structure disregarding formality. The whole structure is covered with a soft touch and simple and fresh colour; then we add a warm and bright spring mood to it. In the end the atmosphere of spring Ikebana is made.

24. Shoka
Flax lily · Cornflower/Glass vase

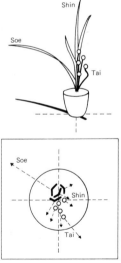

Figure shows the location of Sashiguchi, or insertion points and how to stretch branches.

Like a Light Snow (22)

Looking at this Ikebana, the arranger makes a band of floral plants' root, and puts it into a vase. The technique to give a feeling of veil with gypsophila flowers and keeping the view balance of length and depth by haunting star-lily through the veil, are important points on the structure. The star-lily which is hanging down in this way is one of the most effective branches in the whole structure.

With Early Spring Sunshine (23)

What Ikebana expresses is not always the floral plants shape itself. Through the shape of flowers we try to find out the environment that nurtures plants. The tendency is seen especially in Shoka. Two tulips are arranged as Shin and Soe, and we may find spring sunshine stretching out of the two stems and the inclination of flower's neck. A trace of the endurance, on the bottom leaves' shape, against coldness makes the stretching stems more impressive.

If we prefer the flower which will bloom from a bud, we may express the decisive moment of flowers. The location to show it is Shin flower of tulip. Through arranging a bud as Soe, the very moment in time process becomes clearer.

Childish Dream (24)

From the lemon-yellow glass which looks like emulsified fruit juice, purple, indigo and pink cornflowers are standing up. The harmony of variety in soft touch makes us remember childish dreams. Looking at the flax-lily leaves which are standing up along the side of cornflower, the twig is curved little bit to the right and the Soe leaf is bended deeply to the left; however the delicate response of cornflower in the edge of the main branches expresses its life process. The flexibility in the bending of stems and leaves shows us the beauty of Shoka.

25. Nageire
   Star-lily · Decolourized fern · Plasticized dead-branch/
   Cobalt narrow neck jar

   *When Ikebana shows selfsupportedness with ease, it looks
   like an organic body which has life.*

26. Shoka
Spiraea · Pink/Turkish blue wave shaped and broad vase

41

Through realizing the process of life, Ikebana is created. The form of creatures is classified in to three; that of standing still by selfsupport, of overflowing from the inside, and of affecting outsiders with one's own will. In the case of creatures, even the form of standing by itself is not state of repose. It is the state that one expects one's future and supports oneself. Ikebana is to be formed with the mind which is resonant with the arranger's own desire born out of the plants' form.

Standing on One's Own Legs (25)

Decolourized fern and plasticized little branches are divided once to the right and the left, and both point to the center and give balance. What is important for this Ikebana is the impression of star-lily looking from the center back. If we arrange the star-lily to one side, the structure is not so much different from the former one, but the emphasis is much different. We feel the powerfulness of life supported by itself from the collective power on the lower back scene.

Stream (26)

When we observe the deed of a great man, we feel something overflowing from the deed. We see the branch streaming in space among plant branches. In Ikebana, to make the branch is difficult, and we call the special technique NAGASHI or streaming a branch. Nagashi is connected with content more than with form. When the main body indicates its self-supportedness and the elevation of the substance shifts the balance of power, the branch takes naturally the form of Nagashi.

The spiraea extended in

Observing from the side because it is arranged for the decoration of shelf, whole body is inclined to the front.

27. Moribana
    Little mulberry vines · Miliocratas · Dendorobium/
    Square vase with strange ears

accordance with distortion of the vase is rising as Shin branch, while a pink with a crimson shade is showing a beautiful tension at the water's edge along the spiraea. Then the tension of pink as faint as heart throbbing with joy creates the generous stream of spiraea. The beautiful impression of arranger results from the floating shape of pure white flower in space being supported by the flexibility of branches.

Movement (27)

We are surprised to see the strong will of plants which appear even unmovable at a glance. When an object which has a power to stretch out encounters a kind of resistance, its will is recognized. When the tops of the mulberry vines are cut off and arranged in the vase an unusual energy of life is revealed in the vines, as a fresh green miliocratas and a dendorobium are placed at the edge of the water.

43

29. Nageire
   Torch-azalea · Pine-tree/Yellow jar with curved ears

*Each shape of a plant indicates its own strength. Further-
more, the strength changes over the years and with the seasons.
The various schools of flower arrangement result from a special
emphasis on a certain aspect of the changes in the strength. For
example, the emphasis in Ikenobo School has long been freshness and simplicity.*

Purity (28)

A gregarious rabbit-ear-iris which has various purple blooms and buds in its green leaves is very beautiful. When each of the leaves is individually observed stains and other imperfections are noticed in them. Nevertheless, the beauty of the gregariousness lies in the purity of life. In Ikebana of the rabbit-ear-iris the principal object is placed on deriving this beauty. When the beautiful part of the gregariousness is intensely focused, the stains and other imperfections become un-noticeable. The use of three combined leaves as Tai is a good example to show the "personal history" of the rabbit-ear-iris; A blossom partially shown from behind the leaves indicates the typical position of the flower of the rabbit-ear-iris of April. In other words a group of Shoka is arranged to bring out the symbol of the gregariousness.

Just Now (29)

The arrangement of Ikebana actually begins with selecting its materials. The colour and the shape of floral plants have a close relationship to the very essence of the plants. Spring flowers and plants are vividly filled with freshness and youthfulness. A new spring branch and stem show no trace of snow and frost of winter. Furthermore, they reveal the quick pace of their growth. There is much difference in impression between a full-bloomed flower and a post-full-bloomed flower. Even a crimson coloured flower begins to fade after it reaches its full bloom. Then the flowers and plants obtain the growth momentum, they begin to attain the fullness of life.

The brightness and gorgeousness of the full-bloomed azalea are filled with the joy of this very moment in which the fullness of life which enters into plants as they obtain the growth momentum.

When the green pine-tree is added to it, it becomes more brilliant. If we make the tension climax just before the balance between the azalea and the pine-tree breaks, the joy of that moment appeals to us powerfully.

Flower in a Time (30)

The rabbit-ear-iris which continues blooming in accordance with four seasons can be adopted to the lapse of time or the accent of its life, into the structure. The Japanese iris, however, shows the overflowing of a single life as the "flower in a time". It blooms high at Shin, and the buds are ready to burst. The overflowing of life makes for flexibility of the leaves' top in a rabbit-ear-iris, while it becomes the potency of spearing Heaven in the case of a Japanese iris.

30. Shoka
    Japanese iris/China jar
    with vertical stripes

Japanese Iris   Rabbit-ear-iris

Difference of leaves composing

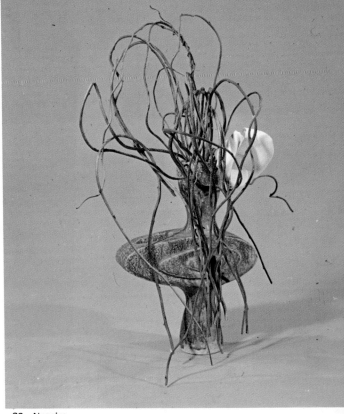

32. Nageire
   Wistaria's vines · Calla/Green top-shaped jar

Ikebana is breathing in space. It occupies space in such a manner that Ikebana seems to disintegrate when it stops breathing. The space surrounded by Ikebana differs from that surrounded by walls; it is the space through which wind blows.

◀ 31. Nageire
   Striped cast-iron plant · Allium/Two tops jar

Liveliness in Space (31)

When slits are artificially made on the leaves of the cast-iron plant along the veines of the leaves, an unexpectedly interesting shape is revealed in space. The stems and leaf behind the slits create a beautiful illusion when they are seen through the slits, just as many objects do when they are seen on a mirror or through a lens. Even though these artificially created illusions deviate from their natural appearance, they reveal astonishing freshness. A certain faculty residing within the heart of man enables him to enjoy illusions and phenomena totally unrelated with reality. This faculty bridges reality to the future.

The wine-coloured allium seen through the artificial slits on a leaf of the cast-iron plant creates a mysterious beauty like a phantom. Several spaces formed by the cast-iron plants in the front and the back in accordance with various visual angles are livelily interwoven; furthermore, they focus on the single position of the allium.

Calmness in Space (32)

When the enclosed space are formed by the lively wisteria vines, a qualitative difference is revealed between the enclosed spaces and the outerspace. The enclosed spaces reveal the appearance of vacuum of the absence of tension in which complete clamness rests. The focal point of Ikebana in this case does not lie in emphasizing the intricately entangled complexity of the wisteria vines but in bring out a collection of the enclosed spaces each of which reveals to our eyes the openness of space as well as the liveliness of the vines. Particularly when a short allium is placed in this extended area, the vines' intence liveliness, with which the vines make a transition from a calm rest to an active movement is created.

Movement in Space (33)

The arrangement of the slit three leaves of the cast-iron plant from the left to the lower right side reveals the flow of a breeze. The appearance of a soft current of the air breezing from the left side to the right. A strange flower appears (actually it is tulip whose petals are bent outwardly) to be protected by

33. Moribana
    Aspidistra · Tulip/Conduit shaped vase with three legs

the cast-iron leaves and to be bathing in the spring sun.

This Ikebana is thought to be placed in the environment of the warm spring sun rays descending from the upper right side and of the soft current of the open air breezing from the left to the right. Ikebana begins an eternal breathing under the spring sun and in the cool breeze which are created in a simple arrangement of the common materials.

34. Shoka
Tree-paeony/Milk yellow glass

Tree-peony reveals calmness and gorgeousness while the iris shows purity and strength. In Shoka dignity is sought in the shapes of flowers and plants. The degree of dignity revealed in the arrangement corresponds to that in the arranger.

35. Shoka   Floral Iris · Riverside Pink/
            Crests painted white and broad jar   53

Catching Special Character (34)

The beauty of the tree-peony is accentuated by emphasizing the "singleness" of the flower. Because of the surroundings that support it and of the tension created by its self-control, gorgeous flowers appear to be noble. The young leaves that appear to be embracing the flower, the position of the flower that slightly extends over the edge of the water, and the stems that reveal its passage of many years supports the special feature of the beauty of singleness of the tree-peony flower.

Catching Special Phase (35)

The beauty of the floral iris lies in freshness of its flowers, all of which bloom almost simultaneously, and in the strength revealed in the straight leaves and stems. The arrangement of the iris in conformity with the traditional rules would not create the freshness of the plant. It is extremely important that the unique feature of the plant be recognized. For instance, the smoothness and elegance of the straight leaves and stems are clearly exposed when a slight curve is given to them and a small cute plant is placed at the foot of the iris. The discovery of the unique feature of flowers and plants is essential in bringing out their freshness and beauty in their arrangement.

Rich Expression of Scene (36)

A short poem abundantly describes a wide scene by a few words. Similarly, Ikebana-particularly Shoka-must be able to reveal the natural scene used as its background. For example, the arrangement of the wheat plants should ideally express the May sky full of the bright sunshine and nice smell. This implicit description in the arrangement of the natural scene expose the beauty of Shoka even more concretely.

The position and the direction of the tops of the ears of wheat, together with the almost equally tall cornflower placed closely with the wheat remind us of field scenery of May in which the plants are acceleratedly growing into the sky. Since the stems of the wheat and cornflower plants appear to have exhausted their growth potentials, they reveal no power in them. Therefore, our visual interest naturally shifts from the stems to the tops of the ears of wheat which help us discover the feelings of the May sky behind them used as the background. A technique employed in this arrangement is Mazeike or mixed arrangement.

36. Shoka
   Wheat · Cornflower/Crests painted white and broad jar

37. Shoka
Amaryllis/Green vessel with circle crests

    One of the crucial points in Shoka arrangement lies in the "naturalness" of the plant or flower inherent in them. For example, it is important in arranging the amaryllis, narcissus and rhodea to let the inherent quality — either in the impression revealed by the general outline of the plants as a whole or the impression revealed by each leaf or flower of the plant — guide the entire arrangement. It is the arrange-structure connoting the growth process of the plant that reduces the distance to the truth of creation.

This Moribana is composed centering around the beauty of the amaryllis flower and the back scene of Ikebana not only enhance the colours and shapes of the plant but also gives a stability to the arrange-structure. For example, the almost unnaturally declining amaryllis which appears about to fall is visually stabilized by the flax-lily leaves. As a result the impression of the unstableness from the unnaturally declining amaryllis disappears and strangely enough, a certain mood is revealed from it.

38. Moribana
Amaryllis · Flax-lily/Compote shaped ceramic with ears

In arranging Ikebana the efforts to retain and/or reveal the inherent quality have brought about several traditional rules of the thumb. For example, in arranging the pine tree and the Japanese plum tree it is said, "the arranger must learn about their qualities from the pine trees and the plum trees in the natural environment, the woods." However, even if the arranger retains the individual shapes and other features of the plant that it had before it was cut off from the natural environment, the woods, the arrangement fails to reveal and/or retain its inherent qualities or the impressions from the qualities. In Ikebana, the quality of a plant can be divided into two: the one is the inherent or innate quality that is unchangingly embraced in the plant since its birth, the other is the "natural" quality that changes in accordance with the changes in the natural environment in which the plant breathes. Without the former the latter cannot be sensed; without the latter the former cannot be observed. When these two types of quality is skillfully combined in arranging Ikebana, the life, freshness and beauty of the plant are more truly revealed.

To Know Origin (37)

The flowers and plants have their own growth patterns. When the life of plants is observed in a certain point of their time table, the new leaves are growing longer than the old ones on some plants and vise versa on some others; and some plants have the flowers on the lower branches and the flowers on the twigs. The careful observation of the plants in their growth-time table enables an arranger to attain a clearer expression in Ikebana and a broader domain of the expression.

This Shoka tries to catch the originality of the amaryllis which is one flower in one stump, having the flower stem in the center and the flower stem growing taller as the bud opens into full bloom. In spite of little changes in the life of this plant, the amaryllis' Shoka reveals a fresh season and joy with which the plant meets a new point of time passage.

Like Nature (38)

Ikebana, which is arranged freely in space, does not create

its back-scene within the arranged form itself. But there are occasions in which a part of the arrangement-form is used as a certain type of a back-scene so as to accentuate a focal point of the expression in the arrangement. This technique is adopted to strengthen the impression of a part of the plant. It is used not for simply accentuating the colours and shapes but for revealing the inherent quality of the plant.

The amaryllis usually blooms on the upright stem. If the plant bends it loses its stability. Even if physical stability is attained in the arrangement an obvious instability can be sensed from the view-point of the "living" plant. In Ikebana of the amaryllis the bend on the top the leaves and the prone flower creates a certain sense of stability, an element of life and sentimentality.

A stump is formed by placing the flower stem in the center of the structure and letting three leaves face each other. The long leaf in the front plays a role of Tai or body. The flower in the front should be one that gives the impression of weakness or delicacy.

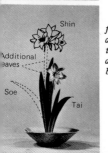

A different stump is formed by placing two additional leaves behind the flower and sticking a tall flower as Shin behind them.

59

Ikebana in Summer

The breezy early summer is followed by a hot mid-summer in which we particularly enjoy water and the shade of trees. Enduring severe sunshine flowers bloom and trees thrive. In spite of the intense mid-summer heat flowers please our eyes and the greens comfort our hearts. In the mid-summer sometimes passionate flowers can be found; however in Ikebana of the mid-summer flowers and plants, refreshing and restful arrangements are sought. The summer Ikebana seeks simplicity in its composition and clarity in its expression which can create a cool and refreshing atmosphere.

39 Moribana
Gerbera • Plasticized Branches/Boat shaped purple glass

40 Shoka
Gladiolus/Wine glass shaped china

With Simplicity (39)

The gerbera carelessly placed in a vase lets its simple flowers bloom and still retains the pace of growth in its stems. Observing the gerbera as almost synonimous with a rapidly growing child you find a certain unexpected sentiment when the plant is arranged in the vase. Needless to say there is a unique impression from the light coloured flowers; something in these interesting stems appeals to our heart. This interesting phenomena becomes even more impressive by adding the plasticized little tree with its white granules to the gerbera. The youthfulness and simplicity are accentuated by placing the two heterogenious plants side by side in the vase. The feeling of coolness is well effectuated by parting the two plants at a distance sufficient to avoid the feeling of crowdedness in the vase.

Full of Vitality (40)

The freshness of the gladiolas is shown by the colour of its flower. Its pink petal begins to fade as it blooms more fully. The different degrees of the colour (pink) intensity in a group of flowers enable us to sense the existence of the vital life in the plant. The stems that take in the water face up toward the light in a short time after they are placed in the water. One of the best of Shoka is to arrange the fresh and lively gladiolus in the simplest of forms. The gladiolus gives us the impression that it will continue to grow taller step by step as the blooming is completed from the bottom to the top. The slender stems supported by the leaves embracing the flowers, reveal their earnest life and a proper amount of tension with which it braces its life.

Green and Young Leaves (41)

In the shade of the green trees the cool wind is gently blowing and the dewdrops are rolling off the leaves. The light-green of the leaves appears much cooler and more refreshing than an elegant flower. The lily flower under the shade of the green maple is full of a poetic mood. The softness and the live-liness of the leaves and the white petals with a shade of light green support the feeling of purity and phantasy with which the

41. Shoka
White tranpet lily/
Green compote

lily is filled. The lily should be slenderly and simply arranged by
placing one flower to each of the three positions, namely Shin,
Soe, and Tai. The degree to which the neck of the flowers is bent
is very important. If you bend it as much as it is bent in the
natural environment, the flower will look withered. We bend it
only a little to retain the liveliness and gentleness of the plant.
It is also important in arranging the lily to keep the water surface
uncluttered.

42. Moribana
   Arocasia · Scirpus/Light blue glass vessel

The "elasticity" of delicate thing contains the feeling of smartness. It is kind of well defined Japanese traditional beauty, and also it blends with the modern touch in new circumstances. This Ikebana among the mid-summer Ikebana's creates an atmosphere most conductive to coolness and freshness.

43. Nageire
   Fruit of Lotus · Dahlia · Leaves of Rabbit-ear-iris/
   White bending tube vase

Sharpness (42)

Parts of space in which the arocasia is freely arranged are framed by the sharply bent scirpus. There is no strong and powerful looking plants in this Ikebana. This Ikebana is composed of only a transparent vase, the arocasia's soft leaves which hold gentle plane, and a few straight stems of the scirpus. Furthermore, these plants and the vase have simple and light colours. The important key to the beauty of this Ikebana is to create a feeling of astonishment and a flash of wit from the straightness and the sharpness formed by sharply bending the stems. Also the simple, light colours and the transparency of the vase reveal the feeling of cleanness.

Glossiness (43)

It is a natural arrangement to place a lotus fruit at the opening of the vase in front of the rabbit-ear-iris leaves which are waving tenderly. The plants to be added to this is very limited in colour and shape. An important role is played by a change, in the direction of force, created by a thin dahlia stem and the slant flower, and the colour of the dahlia flower that adds a "gloss" to the Ikebana. The "glossiness" of the living beings is revealed in the form of a delicate balance of force as an additional force (wind's waveness) emerges in the rabbit-ear-iris leaves on the left side as the result of a new force formed by inserting the dahlia extending downward to the right hand. Since we tend to lose "glossiness" and "elasticity" in the summer season, we find unusual freshness and beauty in "glossiness" created in Ikebana.

Elasticity (44)

The freshness of the leaves, and the purple colour of the flowers if the summer rabbit-ear-iris meet the ideals of a summer plant to reveal a cool and refreshed atmosphere, but it is about to lose its inner energy. However, it is still possible to express a refreshing beauty in Ikebana of such a plant by revealing its "elasticity" that is, the sign of its ceaseless growth potential. Addition of the scirpus to the summer rabbit-ear-iris supports this last point very effectively. Furthermore, sharply bent scirpus stem strengthens the growth potential hidden in other stems used as Shin. A slight bend on each leaf reveals the "elasticity" of the plant with which the leaves seem to be returning to a certain focal point.

44. Shoka
Rabbit-ear-iris · Scirpus/
Broad top brown vessel

45. Moribana
   Blue-gum · Mokumao · Castor-bean/Blue T-shaped pottery

This Ikebana reveals God's Love given to us and the endlessness of a long river. A sense of moss of a thousand years is preserved in this Ikebana as a symbol of eternity.

68

46. Nageire
Asparagus · Campanula · Cockscomb/
A couple of bottle neck jars with different colour

*A touch of eternity is revealed by different shades within the
simple colours, softness of the colours, and the spaces, between
the stems and between the leaves, through which a gentle breeze
swims. Expansiveness of heaven is one of Ikebana's beauties very
difficult to express.*

Thicket (45)

The blue-gum and the mokumao are extending smoothly to the right. The caster-bean flowers are seen behind the opening of the vase as if they are trying to check the smooth extention to the right. The crucial point of this Ikebana lies in the combination of two energies, namely, the energy of the blue-gum and the mokumao to grow to the right and the energy of the caster-bean flowers to try to check the first energy. A living plant can be best portrayed simply not by its existence on the soil but by its dynamic growth process in which the living plant keeps springing out of the earth. Just like the endless water of a fountain, a living plant grows continuously with the nursing of a thicket. When we retain scale a dynamic element of a plant in Ikebana the largeness of scale such as eternity can be realized even in a small Ikebana.

Spaciousness (46)

The cross-over of the asparagus ferns from a dark green vase with those from a light coloured vase creates a mood of a smooth expansion into the spacious sky. The spaciousness is created by the campanula and the cockscomb at the opening of the vase. When the movement from thickness to thinness and from darkness to light, is interrupted (by the campanula and the cockscomb flowers in this case) the expansiveness of the asparagus ferns into the vast sky comes to be sensed clearly.

Forcefulness (47)

The perfection revealed individually in the simple and massive vase and in the forceful leaves of the strelitzia and the windmill-palm cannot create the forcefulness of the Ikebana as a whole. Only when each of the materials is given some personality and harmonized with one another in Ikebana is the perfection of the individual plants transformed into the strength of the will of a living being and the Ikebana attains a "scale" larger than the size of the arrangement-form.

47. Nageire
    Strelitzia · Windmill-palm/White ceramic with a crack at
    bottom

   *The seven coloured flower petals contain "elasticity"; the
flower skirts reveal keenness in the strength of the straight
stems. A couple of the strelitzia flowers are facing the same
direction connoting a motion behind which the windmill-palm
extends its leaves flatly with a slight bend in each of them. All
the curves in this Ikebana show a motion toward a point in the
left front. A force, hidden in the simplicity and the clarity of
this arrangement-form, indicating the largeness of the scale
appeals to a man of strong will.*

Ikebana in Autumn

Autumn is the season for plants to bear fruits. Plants and trees attain the penetrating colours and a sense of fullness. In the autumn Ikebana the autumnal colours are to be focused as the fast approaching turning-point of a plant's life.

72   48. Nageire
         Strelitzia · Castor-bean/Two heads jar

49. Shoka
   Balloon-flower/Cubic china jar with fo

Delicate Balance (48)

Ikebana is formed by the conflict and harmony between two forces. The impression of the vivid growth of plants in spring Ikebana is created by showing a lag or difference in growth between the new plant and the old plant, while the autumnal mood is often created by the conflict of two forces. When the two forces conflict Ikebana fully embraces the sense of transiency of the autumnal pathos. There is a certain delicate balance of forces in this colourful Ikebana among (1) the strelitzia extending forward from the rear opening of the vase, (2) the leaf from the front opening of the vase bends backward, and (3) the castor-bean flowers trying to unite the opposing forces between the strelitzia and the leaf. This delicate balance is the foundation to this Ikebana.

After Rain and Dew (49)

The sense of transiency of the plant's life is hidden behind the brilliant purple of the balloon flower. The reason why a balloon-flower cannot reveal the fulness of the autumnal plant's life is that the plant's strength to endure rain and dew has not been built in its branches and leaves. The balloon-flower in Shoka is naturally arranged reflecting its inherent quality. The weakness of the plant is shown on the bending top of Soe and Shin branches and on the curve in the middle. Furthermore, the tendency of the plant to turn toward the sun with dew on the top of its branches reveals the fresh mood of early autumn.

Turning Point of Life (50)

A touch of the autumnal mood is connoted in the fresh appearance of the stems which gives even a cruel and rough appearance, strengthens the freshness of the stem's bark, and reveals a sense of transiency as does the autumnal pathos.

50. Nageire
Water-banana/China jar with ears

The key to this Ikebana lies in giving a little more weight to the light as the balance between the light and shade creates a tension. The combination of both the freshness of the stem's bark and the clear colour of the leaves reveals the beauty of the plant's life along with the sense of transiency of the autumnal pathos.

75

Bright Colour (51)

Among the ananas, the millet, and the vase there is a smooth flow of the gently shifting from yellow to orange. The addition of the fresh green monstera leaf makes this Ikebana very refreshing. Observe the interesting surprise and the effect of the contrast brought out by the green leaf. Also note that the monstera leaf is not totally out of place but that it blends itself well with the other materials here and with this arrangement-form.

Subtle Colour (52)

The red cockscomb, the vermillion coloured miscellaneous wood and the purple coloured branches with the plasticized granules create a smooth continuity to the purple vase. The gentle shifts in the colours, the arrangement-form, and the touch of this Ikebana creats a subtle mood.

51. Moribana
Ananas · Monstera · Millet/Triangle vesse

52. Moribana
Cockscomb · Vermillion coloured branches · Purple
plasticized miscellaneous branches/China jar with two trunks

As autumn nears to its end, a certain tension is observed in the life of grasses and trees. A majestic expression on Rikka and Shoka is created by the conflict and the harmony of two heterogeneous forces. Particularly, late autumn Ikebana requires these manipulation of the forces.

53. Small Composition of Rikka
    Rhapis-humilis-blume · Cockscomb · Oriental-bittersweet · Anthurium · Sunflower · Flax-lily/China jar

54. Nageire
Cockscomb · Strelitzia · Rhapis-humilis-blume/Green
cylindrical china

Creating Harmony (53)

In the way of Rikka the autumnal mood is expressed mainly
by the cockscomb and the oriental bittersweet. The rhapis-
humilis-blume used as Shin and Do contributes to make the
height and the spaciousness of the autumnal sky. The clearness
of this Ikebana results from the harmony between the two
heterogeneous materials.

Good Use of a Gap (54)

The harmony of two heterogeneous materials can be attained
by adding the third material which has something in common
with the first two materials, or which fills the psychological
space created in the gap between the first two materials. A sense
of transiency of the autumnal pathos can be felt in the gap
between the rhapis-humilis-blume and the strelitzia. The
cockscomb maintains the structural balance of this Ikebana.

55 Nageire

Oriental-bittersweet • and Banana /
Two trunks china jar with numerous
short lines

56 Moribana
Dahlia · Millet/Glass vase

As late autumn nears, the colours increase in their intensity and the stains of wind and snow begin to appear on the branches and leaves. We are deeply moved by the sense of transiency of the autumnal pathos. However a "gloss" is required in the autumn Ikebana. "Gloss" for the autumnal Ikebana is not the same as the gloss for the summer Ikebana. "Gloss" for the summer Ikebana embraces coolness and freshness, whereas "gloss" for the autumnal Ikebana connotes the burning of the inner energy of life. The warmth seen in the spring Ikebana is radiated from the outside while the warmth of the autumn Ikebana is radiated from the inner life of the plants themselves in the cold autumnal air.

81

In Sentiment (55)

The human heart is unintentionally embraced by sentiment; therefore, it is often said that sentiment is more or less a dream. Sentiment may have its origin in the future surpassing the here-and-now or in the past. Sometimes we find our comfort in ill-treating ourselves. We experience a new joy when we find a drop of light in our broken heart. Such a sensitivity of our heart can be expressed in Ikebana. The leaf of the water banana is torn and its stem is broken. The oriental bittersweet branches are refractionally running in the sky. In these settings the orange coloured fruits are shining. The warmth of the plant's inner life is about to reach even the twigs. Here, we find a mood of the autumnal sentiment transcending the arrangement-form.

In Nature (56)

The dahlia, which has continued to bloom since early summer changes its colour delicately in accordance with seasons. In a group of dahlia flowers of many shades of red "a colour of life" emerges. When the dahlia flowers are contrasted with the brown millet corn grains and a milk-coloured vase between them, the "colour of life" is even more refreshed. The warmth radiating from the inner life of the plant can be made more impressive with the use of very short stemmed flowers.

In Shape (57)

As it grows colder day by day, the red colour of the ganges-amaranth increases in its freshness. The plant prepares its life to protect against the cold wind and the continuous sunshine days. The form of the Shoka results from a careful observation of Nature, and reveals the warmth the quiet life of plants.

This Ikebana is composed by the way of "HIDARITAI" ▶
(body of the left hand) which is a special arrangement-form in shoka. This arrangement-form is used to follow the natural curve of Shin branch. According to the way of "MAZEIKE" (mixed arrangement) an eulalia is placed in the back as Soe to accentuate the mood of the season.

57. Shoka
Ganges-amaranth · Eulalia/White china with meshy pattern

59. Nageire
Castor-bean/Broad jar with many heads

The colour of the castor-bean resembles that of many things exposed to the setting sun, and conveys a soft mood in this Ikebana. However, the two unproportionally large leaves and their positions reveal forcefulness. There is an element of power-fulness in this simple arrangement-form.

◀ *The inner full strength is revealed in the simplified structure of these retrenched simple materials. Also the impressiveness beyond the nature of the plants is conveyed.*

Suppressed Power (58)

The oriental bittersweet branches are curved in such a way that they encircle the front of the vase. When the top of the oriental bittersweet's main stem is freely extended, it reveals its original character. However, when it is so curved and suppressed, the power, originally exerting on the top, is retained in the stem. In this way a suppression endows Ikebana with an unexpected powerfulness. The branch, that is extending to the right hand, reveals the plant's full resistance against the suppression exerted on the main stem. When a directive sun-flower is placed above the well balanced circle of the oriental bittersweet vine, a strange gap appears and it creates an expression far distant from the inherent character of the plant.

Finding out Secret Expression (59)

As we change a way of arranging the plants, we discover that they embrace a character different from that of the first glance. The shape of the caster-bean leaves connotes a strange sense. In order to emphasize this sense we must place the caster-bean plant in a special setting. When the flowers on a twig are placed between the two large leaves, the contradiction between the two large leaves and the flowers on the twig is dissolved in this simple structure and furthermore this Ikebana appeals forcefully to use.

Expression Made of Quality and Shape (60)

When a single character of a plant is emphasized and the other characters of the plant are ignored in Ikebana an unexpected mood is created. A forcefulness and a deep impression are formed when this mood can remind us of a certain thing that exists in a corner of Nature.

◀ 60. Nageire
Sunflower · Miscanthus/China jar

87

Ikebana in Winter

Winter Ikebana is filled with the plants' longing for spring. A touch of spring is felt in the cold air, and the life of beings to move slowly. Signs of spring to come are at first brought together at one point, and later they spread out. The winter Ikebana's uniqueness lies in the arrangement-structure which is capable of conveying this spreading of signs to the entire body of the plant to tell of the forth coming spring. Occasionally, a bright and cheerful Ikebana is seen in winter. This type of Ikebana in winter is arranged under the assumption that spring has come again in a depressed room of winter. It is thought that these winter Ikebanas embrace the mind of people longing for spring to come.

61. Nageire
Cymbidium · Milliocratus · Synthetic resined pink branches/ Turkish blue china with broad top

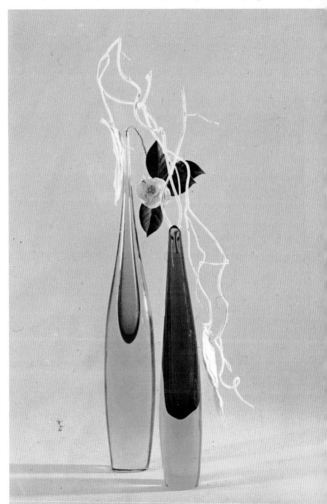

Rose Shining (61)

The green colour is intensified by the pink plasticized small branches, and the flowers of the orchid are refreshed with its "elasticity." Spring begins to gleam in a depressed room of winter.

Cool Eyes (62)

A couple of stream-lined and quiet glass vases are joined by the dry, yet soft bean vines. The Camellia is seen from behind the vines. The tightness and "elasticity" of the camellia as well as the spring colours of the vases convey to us a touch of spring.

Unexhausted Life (63)

Just as water flows under snow, a plant begins its life under its skin. The smoothly curved red-bud-willow stems are embracing a touch of Spring to come soon; the buds on these stems are growing in size at a progressive rate and begin to wear a colour; and soon they will burst into silver furs. The leaves of the winter-chrysanthemum are embracing a shade of red connoting that they have endured many a cold day. The flowers begin to greet the sun. A smooth curve below tightness at the surface of the water (in the vase) conveys unexhausted life. This Ikebana indicates how well Shoka can convey the plant's longing for spring to come. It is crucial that the winter sunshine is expressed through the use of a smooth curve of branches, and the growth of buds and through conveying the increase in the shade of red.

63. Shoka
    Red-bud-willow · Winter-chrysanthemum/White china jar
    Japanese Apricot/Copper jar with ears

◀ *Seeing from the frontage the shoka looks a piece of apricot;
we can, however, find out that the shoka is composed with much
piling branches, when we see it from the side.*

64. Moribana
Camellia · Fern/Triangle vessel with legs

Even in an insignificant scene of winter an unexpected life can be found. A spot of white among the green conveys a sense of purity.

65. Shoka
　　Fenix · Dendrobium/Day-break coloured glass comportier

　　This Ikebana is full of brightness and joyfulness. This noble Shoka contains auspiciousness in abundance.

Keeping Original Intention (64)

Ikebana has not only an ornamental element but also an esthetic sence. The ferns that extend smoothly from the weighty vase express simple, yet vital strength of life. The camellia by the gregarious ferns expresses purity. Here we see a special movement in Ikebana. The original beauty of Ikebana lies in the sense of nobility that results from the modest, yet beautiful movement transformed from an intention of the earth.

Day-break Colour (65)

The colour of the glass vase forms skillfully a soft mood and enables the beauty of the flowers to penetrate into space. The main plant is the dendrobium, and the fenix used as Shin is just an attachment. However, the fenix plays an important role in the arrangement-structure: it adds tightness and strength to the weak dendrobium stem. The narrowness of the lower half of the vase, the height of the vase, and the fenix convey a tightness in elegance and a freshness in splendour. This Ikebana creates freshness seen in the sky of day-break.

Sound of Wind (66)

Beauty cannot be found at a first glance in this Ikebana consisting of a wingled spindle-tree and the fruits of the lotus. Rather, loneliness of winter is revealed in this. When we transcend our mind and heart, there remains only a boundless vacancy. In this state of mind and heart we can hear even the sound of a breeze. At this time we realize a strong will in ourselves. An elastic strength is found in the four gently curved projections of the vase and the twigs of the winged spindle-tree.

66. Moribana
   Winged spindle-tree · Fruit of lotus/China with four horns

In obeying nature, such as withstanding the withering blast of winter's wind, the plant reveals an unblending character in this Moribana. The "elasticity" on the small branches indicates that the twigs are ready to sprout at any moment. When the inner life of the plant displaces the external beauty, Ikebana attains an esthetic mood.

67. Shoka
Narcissus/Bamboo barrel

The passage of time from winter to spring is revealed in the white petals contrasted against the dark green leaves. Pureness is connoted by the fine powder on the white petal's skin. The inner life of the narcissus is momentarily perfected in four leaves facing each other and the flower fully blooming.

CONTENTS

FORMATION OF IKEBANA

In order to arrange better Ikebana we should carefully choose a flower which we estimate highly, and look for those elements which compose the beauty. We should watch the direction of branches, the power of the main stem and the root which keep the balance, the expression of the leaves concentrated toward the light source and the various colors of the flowers. Then we should look for a reappearance of those elements which we inspected. The simplest order of plants is that the direction of branches and leaves is carried away by the light. Keeping that in mind, we decide on a vase, fix the direction of stretching flowers and leaves, and give pleasing proportions as to size, strength and curve to each shape. We, however, should learn the fundamental structure of Ikebana, in order to make authentic forms.

Main Branches in an Ikebana Composition

Any Ikebana is composed of three main branches. If there is no single outstanding branch, an arrangement is said to be made of three parts. Even complicated compositions are made of three branches or parts. Such parts or branches are combined like chains and broadened repeatedly. The concept is an abstraction and formalization of the shape of growing plants. The concept is explained in terms of IN-YO-GO-GYO. We shall consider this concept and its explanation from the viewpoint of Ikebana.

Thinking about all phenomena in the world, we realize that one origin is divided into two powers. Phenomena are produced by various connections between these two powers. One of these powers is called IN, and the other is YO. They attract and repulse each other and move continuously to and fro just as the poles in electricity or magnetism. All phenomena are born and become active through this concept. Life begins when minus turns to plus. It is filled with fresh vitality by the movement of plus, then it blooms and calls butterflies. When life passes over the climax, it turns to minus. It leaves seeds for new development, however, and then returns to complete minus there to wait for spring. In this way the repeated variations between IN and YO contain the melody of life, and produce the rises and

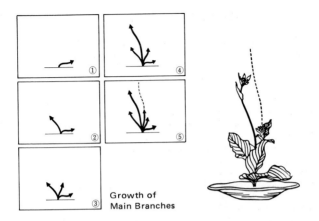

Growth of
Main Branches

falls of activity. Life is YO; death is IN. Light is YO; darkness is IN. In flower arrangement one should sense a fresh stretching, a vivid rising, a healthy tension, a shining joy and the sense of waiting for spring from the rising and falling of IN and YO, because this is the original intention expressed in the melody of IN and YO. In arranging flowers, the human being exists and believes in the possibility of the future, and the power and intention of life through obedience to the laws of IN and YO. If we suppose YO as heaven and IN as earth, man is situated between heaven and earth; there he relies upon today and hopes for the future in obeying the order of heaven and earth.

When the foregoing concept is applied to branches constructing Ikebana, the first branch rises up high and shows the influence of heaven, the second branch lies down and shows that of earth, while the third stands out above the others and indicates man's intention and the ground of phenomena. These three play the roles of heaven (Soe), earth (Tai) and man (Shin).

Each of the three branches is different in size, weight, strength, speed of growth and direction. In them should be expressed the shape of continual variation and growth. An origin develops to two powers, IN and YO, each of which is quite contrary. Development can not be expected, however, if IN and YO are balanced with the same strength. When the balance is broken, a vivid movement is born. The JIN (man) branch which shows movement, stretches high while leaning sometimes to earth and sometimes to heaven. But development does not stop there. When the JIN branch stretches it joins with heaven or it touches earth and fades on the tone of the strength of earth and new movement begins. In this way development goes from two to three to five to seven. The relation is ever taken as an incomplete form. Consequently we can take plants which exist in a variety of circumstances and overcome those circumstances by expressing them in a form that is an attempt to complete them in their own lives. Ikebana are composed in the ratio of seven, five and three as the reflection of the relation of its parts.

Form of Ikebana

The concrete form of Ikebana is decided by the shape of the material plants and the viewing position. When we look at trees and plants, we realize that the shape of plants is tied to their leanings toward light. Plants have a front and back which are induced by light and they stretch their leaves and bloom their flowers toward light. When we look at plants, they look most beautiful and impressive if we stand with the light source to our back. If we stand a little bit back we may enjoy the shape of plants much better and we may discover their original loving beauty. The locations of flower, light and viewer is fundamental in composing Ikebana.

The shape of material plants varies from stretching to creeping to bending and curving. In accordance with the shape of the material we pick out a vase and decide on location and shape. From this the many sorts of Ikebanas are born.

Nageireru (throwing-in) Style

When we stick a flower in a vase, it is easiest and most natural to lean the flower against the top of the vase. We do not always obtain the beauty we expect but it is simple and natural looking,

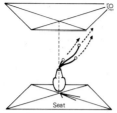

Relative Position of Flower,
Light and Viewer

especially if the branches are stabilized in keeping their surface upward. Looking at the growing shape of trees and plants, we see they rise upwards together. Shaded or side branches, however, stretch diagonally. Leaning against the top of the vase or stretching diagonally are the most natural poses of plants.

At such times, the container plays the role of the main stem in natural plants, and the flower stem which is arranged to keep in line with the supporting force looks stable.

The reason why a flower looks vivid is that its branches and leaves have a self-supporting energy. One technique of flower arrangement is such an expression of energy through shape. If we leave the material free, the tops of branches bend down, and the material looks withered. A fundamental light source should

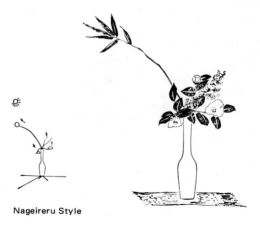

Nageireru Style

101

be imagined and branches fixed toward the light.

Moru (piling) Style

The Nageire style is formed naturally when we put flowers in a jar or a barrel-shaped container. The Moru style is adapted to a broad and shallow dish or a bowlshaped container. If we want to arrange a long branch in the Moru style, we have to learn the arranging technique. Though it is really in the piling style, we use comparatively long materials for making the most of a plant's nature. We should learn the techniques of fixing floral branches freely in a container.

The Moru style is difficult for expressing plant nature. It is possible, however, to make good use of branches in every direction. Once we learn the technique we can show the nature of plants in Moru style just as in the Nageire style. Further the Moru style is suitable for making good use of the beauty of a plant's quality and colour.

Tateru (standing) Style

If we put flowers in a tall and thin container, the plant shows a standing shape. With broader top containers, however, it is hard to arrange freely. This style thus requires much more tech-

Moru Style

Tateru Style

nique than the Nageire style. In spite of this, it was from the Tateru style that Ikebana developed. The reason is that Ikebana was arranged first with a sense of "grasses rising in a swamp" or "planting a tree in a garden."

It is natural for plants to reach up toward the sky. We see the stream of growth there. We feel relieved to see the Tateru style because we can touch the originality. It is as looking at a simple and pure child. Furthermore, the Tateru style leads our eyes from above to below in accordance with the current of the plant, and we sense a nobility much as when we look up at high mountain.

Since the Tateru style is suited to the original nature of plants it looks relaxed and noble. We could call it the "tall shape". It has been esteemed highly as an important beauty in Japanese literature and the theatrical arts.

Rikka and Shoka have been developed from this style and it has developed various techniques and has been formalized for arrangement.

Nageire style has a hospitality and loveliness of floral plants and Moru style has a rich sense and wide space. Tateru style has a nobleness and a carefulness. On the subject of form in Ikebana we usually mention Nageire, Moribana, Shoka and Rikka. Development from these leads to a modern new style which is trying to be born. The Moru, Nageireru, and Tateru styles are not always necessarily only what they are named. In each of the different styles there are elements of the piling or standing shapes. Flowers are arranged in a style fitting the materials, the container, the environment and the idea. For that reason we have to learn the special qualities of the three styles.

HOW TO ARRANGE NAGEIRE

①

Shape of Nageire

As mentioned before, Nageire starts from the natural pose which comes from sticking flowers in a vase, and develops into a shape which enhances the beauty of the materials used. The reason why assembling different flowers in one container does not look unnatural is that the whole body of the arrangement gives us the feeling of a unified will attempting to move toward the same light and breathe the same air.

The unification is carried away toward a spot to the upper right or upper left at the front of the vase. The spot is the focal point assumed by the arranger. It corresponds to the direction of light in natural circumstances. We replace the order of nature by that unification. Except when trying for some high-lighted effect, the focal point in both Nageire and Moribana is located usually to the upper left or upper right at the front. Depending on this, the flower branch heads in that fixed direction. The location of the spot is decided by reference to the bending of the main branches. They do not bend in the same direction. It is necessary therefore to learn the techniques of sticking branches in different directions bending them and turning the direction of leaves. Looking at the above composition we see the direction of the rose leaf to be bent slightly with contrary leaves out away.

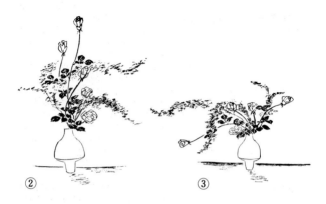

② ③

Asparagus leaves are also put in order according to their natural bending.

The three figures on these pages are examples showing how the shape of flowers is varied by the location of the focal point. The first is the most common form. The focal point is assumed to be in the upper right and all branches have an intention to run to the focal point in soft curving. The second expresses an intention to have the focal point located at the left top. The third assumes the focal point left and low and a few branches stretch to the left keenly. The arranger corrects the torn shape by inserting branches which stretch to the right, and he tries to keep the balance by bending the top of the right hand branches a little bit to the left.

Form of Flower and Shape of Container

The location of the focal point takes on a relation to the shape of the container and to the stability which comes from that shape because the container carries away the bending of the branches. Bending or curving branches which are stretched from the standing main stem do not look unstable even if they lean to one side, unless they go against the original shape of the branches. The container is sufficient if it supports the up and down energy. When branches stretch themselves in bending from the top of a jar, the container should be stable enough to play the role of the main stem. Generally speaking, when the focal point is located downward then branches lean heavily and the container should be much more stable. In the same way, if a container is very stable then the focal point can be leaned heavily. When we arrange flowers in an unstable container we have to assume the focal point to be on the upper side near the center because the shape appears to be moving up. If not, we have to give the directions of branches variety to keep the balance in every direction, and to unify shapes with the focal point through the leaning of the tops of leaves or flowers.

Form and Content

As we see from the illustrated figures, three Ikebana express different sentiments though their materials are the same roses. In reference to the general beauty of the rose, the first figure is the most appropriate form, and it reveals mainly the original elegance of the rose. The second concentrates on showing the growing energy however and the third expresses its bewitchment. If we were to talk about the age of the flower, the second would be young, the first would be moving to meet its climax and the third would be about to pass over its best season. Ikebana is thus not only able to make form but can also provide content. Furthermore, Ikebana should be an expression of the momentary shape which growing floral plants show in the time process.

Fundamental Composition

Nageire starts from a natural pose which is made by placing a flower branch in a vase, and it develops into a form which encourages the beauty of the material. Form has an important meaning in keeping the original growing shape of floral plants, and the arranger should not merely stick a flower into a vase but should try to keep the sense of the flower rising from the vase.

The spot from where a flower branch departs from a vase is

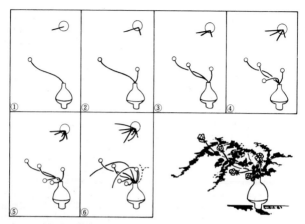

Order of Composition and Location of Branches

called the SASHIGUCHI, and it is in the sashiguchi that we place the first branch. The direction of the second branch is determined by its stretching in response to the shape of the first branch, and the direction of the third is induced from the shape of the second. Looking at the above figures it is seen that the first branch stretches with a mild curve toward the light source and the second is induced from the line of the first. Indeed, the first bends from the arranger's intention. When the second is induced, the intention becomes clear. If we feel there is something wrong in the composition then we attempt to correct it as we place the third branch. As the material of Ikebana has inherent shapes and special colors, we may not always be able to compose just as we plan. It is necessary to adjust and modify in accordance with the state of the flowers or branches. For example, when we put the first branch in with a stretching up to the left, we put the second to the right, and if the first is towards the front, the second moves to the back. We should place the branches alternately starting from the branch which is easiest and must remember to keep good balance. Different branches bend in different directions, and yet each shows an inclination to move toward the focal point. Branches should be arranged so that the whole body appears to bend to and appeal to the observer.

Arrangement of Main Branches

The leading branches in the main parts of Ikebana are called Shin, Soe and Tai, and the supporting branches of these three main branches are called Ashirai. Each floral plant branch varies in strength, length, bending and the shape of its flower and leaf. This makes it simple to compose various Ikebana only by changing the direction slightly. In reference to the arrangement of the main branches, however, we offer the three examples of the next page. Just as we mentioned in the example of the rose of the next page, the bending or curving of main branches varies according to whether they are rising, or drooping styles. We call the rising style Chokutai, bending style Shatai, and the drooping style Suitai. Thus nine fundamental forms are born. If we apply the form to concrete examples, we see in the next page's A and B. In the A arrangement Soe comes to the left more than Shin, and in the B arrangement Shin comes to the left more than Soe. When we put the focal point on the right hand side, the form becomes just the opposite.

Length of Main Branches

When we arrange flowers, we first take the flower branch and remove withered or drooping parts. Inspecting the branches one by one from every angle, we think about the contents of expression, the container and the place where we are to set the composition. Then we plan the construction while considering the shape of the materials. After those preparations we cut away miscellaneous and obstacle branches and trim the main branches.

In accordance with the contents which we want to express, we refer to the main stalk of a composition as Shin. The Shin branch is about one and one-half times the height of the

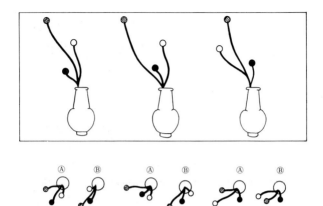

Fundamental Arrangement of Main Branches

container to which is added the width of the container. Next we take the branch which is the second strongest and arrange it in opposition to the shape of Shin. Its outer length is three-fourths that of Shin. Lastly we place the Tai branch which is shorter but which has the power to the entire arrangement. Tai is half the length of Shin. It is not always necessary to place branches in the order Shin, Soe and Tai. From the branch easiest to place and shape we arrange the branches one by one while maintaining balance. At this time we must not forget that branches are not to be merely placed but must rise up from one point of the vase. If the top of the vase is covered by branches or leaves the composition looks oppressive. It is thus a rule that the placement point comes to one side of the vase top. Because the focal point is fixed a little bit on one side and the whole shape of Nageire bends to that side, the focal point falls to the left or right front of the vase top.

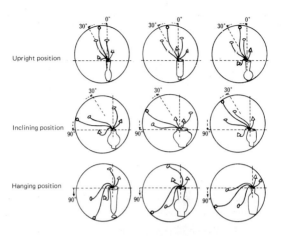

Upright position

Inclining position

Hanging position

Fundamental Types of Nageire

As we see from the above, the fundamental length of Shin, Soe and Tai does not follow the ratio of seven, five and three. We should achieve the ratio (7.5.3), however, because Soe and Tai look shorter through their curving and bending.

When we finish arranging the supporting Ashirai branches and the outline of Ikebana is almost completed, we add more Ashirai to the unbalanced parts, cut away the meaningless intrication of branches and dense parts and adjust the form by bending or straightening the small branches.

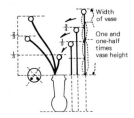

Length of Main Branches and
Fundamental Insertion Point

Reforming of Branches

Reforming of branches is one of the most important techniques in Ikebana. Since material branches are not always suitable to the plan in shape, we sometimes have to bend a straight branch or straighten a bending one. It is often neccessary to change the direction of leaves and flowers. If branches and leaves have an elasticity, it is hard to bend and keep a branch straight. The knack of reforming branches is to bend them as much as possible. In reforming branches we should fix our arms to the side of the chest, place the top of the thumbs on the part to be reformed and then push from both sides and bend repeatedly with little pressure. Just before the branch breaks we release the pressure and the branch is reformed. Weak branch should be bent with a sense of twisting so that the branch will not break. Practice in reforming will help one to understand the quality of each different plant and how best to treat it. Do not attempt to reform weak parts such as knots, or junctions.

Success in the reforming of sticky branches is obtained by bending alone. Moreover, pliable leaves such as narcissus, rabbit-ear-iris, sweet fiag, and others are reformed easily by stroking them as they are held between the middle finger and the forefinger. Good Ikebana natural and exposes less of the reforming process.

Reforming of Branches

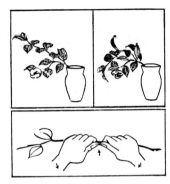

Fixing of Branches

If we merely place floral plants in a vase just as they are, they stand straight when a narrow vase is used and stand diagonally when a broad mouth vase is used. Resultant Ikebana, however, are disunified in form. Small branches stretch out, flowers are bowed in shape and leaves turn their backs to the

Insertion Point of Nageire

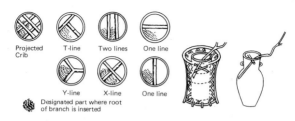

Projected Crib T-line Two lines One line

Y-line X-line One line

Designated part where root of branch is inserted

Partitioning

focal point. Moreover, it is necessary to fix branches in a vase because arrangements lose their shape through winds or vibrations. It is not possible, therefore, to compose the free style we want unless we are familiar with the techniques of how to fix branches.

There is no decisive rule or way for fixing branches in the Nageire style. It is best not to labor in this style so long as the branches are comparatively fast and secure. The method is learned unconsciously but generally complies with the following.

Fixing through Partitioning

The mouth of a vase is partitioned in different ways. In a broad mouth, we fix thin branches one inch down from the mouth of the vase, and insert branches into the part which was narrowed by partitioning. According to the width of the vase and the size and quantity of branches, we adopt either one line, two lines, X-line, T-line or beautifully projected crib lines.

If we use containers which are hard to partition, such as broad mouth jars or bamboo holders, or valuable vases or ones we are afraid to hurt, then we should put a cylindrical substitute which is made of metal or bamboo into the vase and partition the substitute.

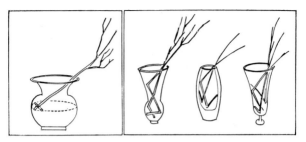

Fixing of T-shaped
Cross Pieces

Fixing through Bending

Fixing through Cutting

With jars or cylindrical containers, branches are sustained and
stabilized using the mouth and the inside wall of the container.
The main stem of the plant, however, is unstable because of its
circular shape. In addition, side branches which usually are
bending often have their surfaces face down. At such a time we
must cut the root diagonally and fix the cut part to the inside
wall of the container. This is the fundamental fixing method of
Nageire. If this method is still not enough to fix a flower or plant
then we often have to use it together with the bending method
or with the T-shape cross-pieces.

Fixing through Bending

When we want to sharpen the inclination of a branch, or
place a vertical shape in a slightly broad mouth container or
change the inclination angle or direction to line up the surfaces
of branches, we bend the part of the branch hidden in the
container so that is touches and remains fixed by tension to the
inner wall of the vase. Moreover, we apply this method when we
fix comparatively thin materials, such as supporting branches
and Nejime (bottom materials).

If you break a branch, it is no longer useful. We should bend
it as far as possible while retaining its elasticity and place it as it

Cutting off

touches the inner wall of the container. Since the proportion of inclination varies in accordance with the location of the bending point and the direction of the branch varies with the bending direction, we should ascertain the structure and the state of branches when we adopt this method.

T-shaped Cross Pieces

Using this method, a cross-piece is inserted into a slit in the branch or else tied in a T-shape. This is the best way for fixing branches in Nageire. The method is good for comparatively thick stems or branches, branches with weighty tops, branches with many curves, or unbalanced branches.

Because stabilization is achieved when both ends of the cross-piece rest against the inner wall of the container in the cross-piece method, it is necessary to cut the root of the branch as close as possible to the cross-point. The length of the cross-piece depends upon the weight of the branch top and curve of the inner wall where the branch touches. Furthermore, the inclination of a branch varies in accordance with where it touches the wall of the container, and the direction of the branch changes depending upon the angle at which the cross-piece is titled. Also just as in bending, we must consider our overall plan and the state of the branches themselves.

When the weight of a branch is one-sided we may still determine its direction and stabilize it by lengthening the lighter side

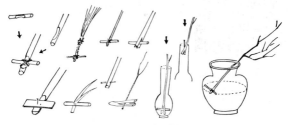

Method of Tying Pieces

Putting Pieces on Legs
and Sticking to Kenzan

Putting Sand on the Bottom
and Sticking to Kenzan

Tying Supporting Branches

of the piece. When a container has a small mouth and we can not fasten the cross-piece securely before inserting it, we overcome the difficulty by splitting the root of the branch and sticking the cross-piece into the split diagonally. Once the branch and cross-piece are inserted they are pressed firmly against the bottom of the container and a T-shape is formed.

When we attach a cross-piece we should consider the many methods available, such as those shown before and make one choice depending on the size, softness or hardness of the flower branches and other factors. If we do otherwise, the branch may turn its direction, or be shaky, and the form of the flower will be broken after the Ikebana is composed.

118

Nageire

Other Methods

When a branch is short and is to be inserted in a deep vase or is too short to sharpen, then we add another small branch to it to lengthen it, bend it with the bending method, and fix it using the T-shaped cross-pieces method. When the material leans to the mouth of a container, and looks unstable because the container is deep, then we put white sand on the bottom of the container. Also, when the top of a branch is too weighty to afford stability we put a Kenzan (needle plate) on the bottom of the container as in the Moribana style, and stick the root of the branch into the Kenzan. There are thus many methods that can be used together. It is important to fix the root tightly as well as to secure a natural and comfortable appearance.

HOW TO ARRANGE MORIBANA

Shape of Moribana

If we faithfully follow the meaning of the word "moru" and pile up flowers regardless of stems and leaves, the result is nothing more than an assortment of materials on a plate resembling what a painter does in a still life painting. What we intend to express in Ikebana is not the beauty of colors and shapes, but the vivid beauty which comes with the growing plant. Most plants preserve their vitality through a shape growing from roots in the earth. In that way, even though we say in Moribana we work with comparatively long branches and leaves, we show the same posture as we do in Nageire arrangements.

The composition is also almost the same as Nageire, and the floral plant stretches up from a point in the container to an assumed point of unification. One different point from Nageire is that materials do not lean to the mouth of a container but stretch up directly from the surface of the water. This is because we use broad mouth containers such as vessels into which water is added. This indicates how the role of containers is different between Nageire and Moribana. Though the container in Nageire often plays the role of the main stem in natural plants, that of Moribana is just enough to support the weight of roots. Furthermore, the container is low and broad at the mouth and appears highly stable. Even if an arrangement leans heavily to one side there is no feeling that the container and all will tip over.

The spot where the branch leaves the water, the MIZUGIWA or water edge, requires a strained feeling. Though the surface of the water is broad, the flower should be arranged so that it rises up from only a part of the surface. The water edge supports the bending of a branch, but gives the appearance that the branch is standing on its own. With this foundation, branches first begin to occupy a wide space and it becomes possible to arrange freely. The general shape and contents of Moribana are not different from Nageire.

Order of Construction and Location of Branches

Fundamental Structure

The exact same structure as in Nageire is shown here. The first branch rises up from the Mizugiwa and has a close relation to the arranger's intention. As we see in the figures right, the first branch of the miscanthus urges the arranger on to creating a fine composition, and the form of the branch decides the structure of the Ikebana.

In accordance with the rising of the first branch, the second branch begins moving. A sharply curved leaf runs after the first branch, and the taste of the miscanthus comes out. The deep curve of miscanthus, however, does not have an inevitability or a decisive taste until the third branch, which is formally located, comes out.

Thus in arranging the fourth and fifth branches, we compose a form of Ikebana

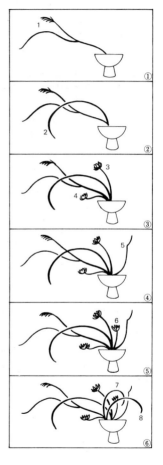

which breathes leniently in space with its own depth and expansion. In that form we find a proportion, a balance, a co-operation, a repulsion, an order and a tone.

Location of Main Branches

Just as in Nageire, the main branches in Moribana are Shin, Soe and Tai. The proportion of power between those three and their separate roles are just the same as in Nageire. The fundamental location of branches is also the same as in Nageire, and the three examples below show the basic styles. The basic styles are divided into the three positions Chokutai (upright), Shatai (inclining), and Shuitai (hanging). Moribana thus has nine fundamental types. Like Nageire, even a basic style in Moribana is applied in two ways through the stretching direction of Shin and Soe. What is different from Nageire is that branches run over a wider space and the number of auxiliary branches is much more than that of Nageire. Consequently, we should pay attention to not missing the effect of space and the sense of growing.

Length of Main Branches

In Moribana as in Nageire the ratio of main the branches' power is basically seven, five and three. While the height of the container is taken as the standard in measuring the length of main branches for Nageire, the width of the container is the standard for Moribana. The length of the Shin branch is one

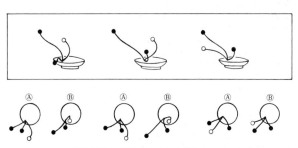

Fundamental Location of Main Branches

Moribana

and one-half times the diameter or length of the container, plus its height. The lengths of Soe and Tai are three-fourths and one-half respectively of the length of Shin. However, these are tentative standards and we are able to change the lengths by intention or by the strength of materials.

In Ikebana, especially in Moribana, we usually bring together several kinds of plants, and the complicated elements are provided for in the combinations of Shin, Soe and Tai. There are short but strong materials, small but sensitive ones, and those with large quantity but less expression. In bringing such elements together, we have to decide on the scale of Ikebana corresponding to the container and attempt to keep a beautiful balance between Shin, Soe and Tai.

As the mouth of the container used in Moribana is wide, the balance between the length of the container and that of the branches varies as the Mizugiwa points vary. The insertion point is sometimes placed in the center of the container, while often

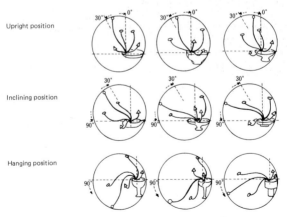

Upright position

Inclining position

Hanging position

Fundamental Types of Moribana

125

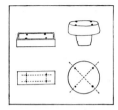

Fundamental Insertion Point

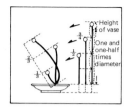

Length of Main Branches

several insertion points are used according to the arranger. Usually, the point is located on the right or left corner of the front or back as the figures shown above. Materials stretch up from the insertion point, the starting point. As the container in Moribana has a wide surface of water it is not good to arrange so as to cover the container. The taste of the plants does not come out and the Ikebana looks gloomy. The key points on producing a fine Moribana are that the materials are to express the tension of growing up from the surface of the water, and the surface of the water is to be exposed as widely as possible.

How to Use Kenzan

To fix branches in Moribana arrangements, Kenzan are used. Actually, many kinds of tools are used but Kenzan is the easiest and the simplest one. It is only necessary to cut diagonally the root of a branch and to stick the root in the needles. Attention should be paid as follows:

1. When we insert branches into Kenzan, we hold the branch root as low as possible and stick it slowly onto the needles.
2. Try not to stick the branches, but attempt to place them between the needles.
3. Be sure to cut the root of branches diagonally and make many splits.

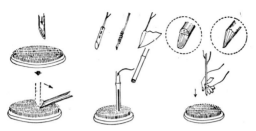

How to Use Kenzan

4. In the case of a thick trunk, cut two-thirds of the root, chip one-third of it diagonally and make splits.
5. With thinner branches or stems wrap the root with paper or cotton. Also, insert paper or cotton in hollow stems such as with dahlias, and then insert between needles.
6. With hollow stems we can also fix a short and thin branch on the Kenzan, and then insert the stem to the branch.
7. When we want to insert a branch diagonally, first insert it straight and then bend slowly. The cut part of a branch faces up and the bark part touches the needles.
8. With sharp curving branches or those with heavy tops, make splits on the bark part or insert a small branch as a pillow.
9. When the top of a branch is too heavy for the Kenzan to support, put another Kenzan upside down on the first one or tie two or three Kenzans together with pieces of material.
10. When a branch is just too big to support with Kenzan, fix it with nails on a piece of wood and place the Kenzan on the wood as shown above.

If we use various methods together, according to what is required, there is more effectiveness. With a deep container we sometimes have to sink sand or stones to the bottom or insert a bottom plate to stabilize the Kenzan.

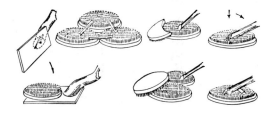

Though it is a speciality of the Nageire and Moribana styles that arrangements can be used briefly, we are also required to learn the techniques of fixing because formative Ikebana is required more and more today.

HOW TO ARRANGE SHOKA

Shape of Shoka

When Shoka first began people arranged Ikebana just as they were growing. Upright plants were arranged as if planted, and bending or drooping plants were placed in hanging containers as they were. Originally, flowers were arranged as offerings to Buddha or for important guests. Shoka itself was born for serving guests, and it provided two branches: one of them for the guest, and the other for the host. As a matter of course the branch for the guest was a bright flower and that for the host a dejected one. Because of the feeling toward guests the flower was required to look clean and vivid.

As people began to realize that flowers were not only beautiful but had living and animated shapes, one of the two original branches got longer and the second became a checking shape on the first one. Two branches thus call to each other, and people use them intending to express the life of plants. In this way the theory that one thing and its opposite together make a phenomenon through their action upon each other was introduced to Ikebana. The form of Shoka which is composed of the cooperation between bright and dark branches, realized this theory. The original form of Shoka was not born until the plus and minus branches appeared.

From that time on these two main branches developed to play a big role while a third branch came to be born at the edge of the water. Thus Shoka came to be composed of three branches. Three branches were arranged with the law of Heaven, Earth and Man and they were named Shin, Soe and Tai. The present form of Shoka appeared through a process of adjustments.

The form of Shoka is much different from that of Nageire and Moribana. In Shoka the container is not a vase but a symbol of the earth. In Nageire and Moribana, the container sometimes symbolizes the earth, but usually it plays the role of the main stem. The role is that of the supporter of a flower stem, or the container of the water which is the nourishment for the material. The reason for the difference is that the contents of expression

129

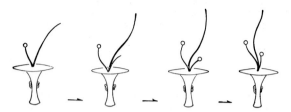

Growth Process to Modern Shoka

is heterogeneous. Nageire and Moribana are composed to reveal the impression of the plant with the partial shape of plants while Shoka is composed to express the ebb and flow of a plant life in organic balance. Therefore, the branch of Shoka rises out of the water edge with a will of being self-supporting. If it stretches up with the support of the container edge as Nageire and Moribana do, Shoka loses its original spirit. Thus the plant which rises up from the symbol of the earth, the container stretches up with elasticity and breathes in space while reflecting its natural shape. As natural plants express shapes according to their surroundings, the material plants of Shoka reveal the shape which was deformed from obstacles but shows a strong will which restores the original quality. It is there we see the spirit which keeps the balance of inner energy as well as that of physical energy.

Fundamental Structure

As we mentioned previously, an assumed point of unification in Nageire and Moribana is found also in Shoka. The point is called Yo, the sun, in Shoka; in other words, it is the same as the natural light source in Nageire and Moribana. As natural plants are deformed by light from one direction only, the shape of Shoka is arranged to be deformed by the influence of Yo. The one difference from Nageire and Moribana is that Yo is set to the back of the flower on the top right or top left.

The realization of this rule has a close relation to the idea of beauty in the Ikenobo School. When this Yo is decided, the fundamental location of branches in Shoka is accordingly solved. The Shin branch, which is in the center and rises up, is first deformed to Yo but shows a strong will to restore the original shape of plants. The Soe branch, which stretches in a bow-shape, extends along the Yo side of Shin and runs to Yo in adding its own movement. The Tai branch, which is a small branch rising up, keeps in balance with Soe and stretches out slightly to the front at an angle. The total form symbolizes the shape of natural plants which rise up from the earth according to the character given by the earth and the order given by themselves. They change their shapes in response to circumstances, and carry the will and hope of growing in their branches. It could be said that the form acquired is a symbolization of the arranger's ideal in daily life.

Location of Main Branches

The general rising shape of young plants is balanced as a symmetrical shape. However, when the wind or light source is from one direction plants change in shape gradually and are deformed naturally in order to maintain a balance between right and left. The inclination to light, especially, is seen on the whole body and on each branch and leaf. We discover a law, however, that inclination to light. The fundamental location of branches for Shoka follows that law. The fundamental form of Shoka is Tateru-Katachi, or the shape of standing which reflects the rising shape of plants. In that shape the light comes at an angle from the rear. The main branch, rising from the center of the container, shows some trace of inclination to light in its growing passage, and in its upper half it inclines to the sun while drawing a lenient arc. This is the shape of the Shin branch. The arc does not run out of the width of the container, but run to the back corner, and the top of the Shin returns to the center of the container.

In fixing the shape of a flower, the deformation of branches and two sides of the flower branch are important to remember.

Changing Phases of Wood

Yo(+) and In(−) of Branch and Leaf

We call the exposed side Hiomote, and the opposite side is called In. These two sides are also called Yonokata (sun-side) and Innokata (shade-side). The Shin branch stretches up in turning its Hiomote to the Yo and gradually extends to the right or left side. Smaller parts are arranged for the Hiomote to be seen from the front. The top of the arc to obtain is set comparatively lower than the middle of the whole Shin length for stabilizing. This is an expression of stretching up with vigor.

Soe is behind Shin and goes along with Shin in turning its Hiomote to Shin. It stretches to Yo in holding Shin. Tai extends to the opposite side of Soe in turning its Hiomote to Shin. Its shade-side is seen from the front.

The original structure of Shoka is the abstraction of a natural plant but the materials of Ikebana are only side branches or small branches of whole plants. We select a suitable branch by referring to the condition of its top and bottom, and its shape

Structure and Location of In and Yo

and strength and then we arrange it like a natural plant.

According to the order mentioned before, we place Tai, Shin and Soe. These three are made up of the master branch and auxiliary branches. As we see in the figures of the next page, 1 is Tai, 5 is Shin, and 8 is Soe. 4 and 6 are auxiliary branches of Shin, and 7 and 9 are those of Soe. The number and place of auxiliary branches rely upon the character of the material, the method of bending, and the contents of expression. Attention must be paid so that the total number of branches flowers and leaves are odd, if they are counted easily.

The auxiliary branches of Shin stand against each other in encircling Shin, and all of them incline to Yo. Those of Soe turn their Hiomote to Shin in surrounding Soe. Those of Tai turn their Hiomote to Soe and gradually turn to Shin as they get closer to having contact with the auxiliary branches of Shin. When all branches, including master branches of course, keep their own will of growing and reveal their inclination to head for the unification point, Yo, we can see the special balance character of Shoka in that Ikebana.

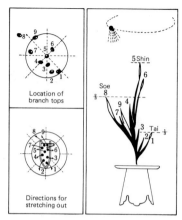

**Fundamental Arrangement
of Branches in Shoka**

Forms of Shoka

Shoka's fundamental form is Tateru-Katachi, standing style. The style varies as a bending, hanging or rising style. In the Ikenobo School we divide those forms into three groups: Shin, Gyo and So. Each may be subdivided again into Shin, Gyo and So to make a total of nine forms.

Shin may be said to be standing, Gyo to be walking, and So to be running. Shin is upright and is a classical form; Gyo is an easy and variable form which is most widely arranged in a standing vessel; So has the most variations and is arranged in a double-decked vessel, a wide mouthed vessel or in a vessel suspended from a wall or ceiling.

Shoka has a close relation with its vessel and the flower form must be chosen according to the shape of the vessel. Therefore, vessels for Shoka are also classified into Shin, Gyo and So. A cylindrical bamboo vessel is a Shin vessel and a wide-mouthed

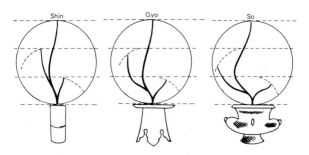

Kagyo (Form of Flower) and Variation of Main Branches

"Usubata" is a gyo vessel. Boats, double-decked vessels, ceiling or wall vessels are So vessels.

The composition with an arc bending to the left is called "Hongatte". If the arc bends to the right it is called "Higatte." Hongatte is the fundamental form of Shoka. In Hongatte, the right is called "In" (darkness) and the left is called "Yo" (light). The Yo is the front and the In is the back. Also, the In is the "Kamiza" (guest position) and the Yo is the "Shimoza" (host position). Since Shoka is used to decorate a Tokonoma, the positions of the Kamiza and Shimoza are fixed.

Kagyo (Flower Form) and Variation of Main Branches

The standard flower form is "So of Shin." The length of Shin is from two to two and one-half times the height of the vessel. The length of Soe is two-thirds of Shin, and that of Tai is one-third of Shin. The width of the arc is the inside of the vessel. Tai goes out to the front but stops inside the vessel. Soe follows Shin, then leaves it gradually at a point a little below the Shin arc top and goes out by the width of the vessel.

The height of Shin, Soe and Tai and the width of the arc vary in accordance with the flower form. As the flower form gets

The First Grade   Flower Forms of Shin
The Second Grade   Flower Forms of Gyo
The Third and the Fourth Grades   Flower Forms of So

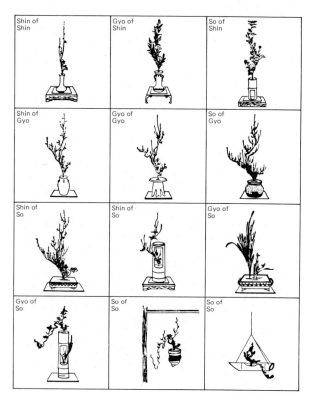

Shin of Shin	Gyo of Shin	So of Shin
Shin of Gyo	Gyo of Gyo	So of Gyo
Shin of So	Shin of So	Gyo of So
Gyo of So	So of So	So of So

Shoka

nearer to Shin of Shin, the arc becomes smaller. Contrarily, as it gets nearer to So, the arc becomes larger. Therefore, the tips of Shin, Soe and Tai, according to the arc, become higher or lower and keep in balance and proportion.

Fixtures

In order to fix the flowers in a vessel, fixtures made of the same material as the flower branch are used. The fixture generally employed is a forked twig. The forked twig of the Rose of Sharon or the staggerbush is most ideal. If the fixture is not firm, the branches will easily fall out of place. One should first, therefore, fit the roots of the flower materials into the forked twig and then cut off the prongs. The fork should then be measured against the width of the vessel, and the base opposite the prongs should be cut just a little longer. The prongs are inserted about three-fourths of an inch into the mouth of the vessel away from the viewer. The base is then pushed in about half an inch. Flowers are inserted in the fork. At the ends, in order to hold the branches in place, a cross-piece is inserted. The base of the fork and the cross-piece should be level in order that the branches be firm.

Kenzan is also used in Shoka. If it is used only for fixing, however, the root looks strange because we expose the water edge in Shoka while we do not in Moribana. We must therefore put Kenzan out of sight by using white sand.

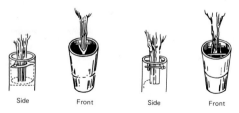

Side   Front   Side   Front

Forked twig   Cross-pieces

Mizugiwa (Water Edge)

The water edge is a special characteristic of Shoka. The roots of branches in the center of the vessel are made to rise in one straight line about two and half inch over the water. Divergence of branches and leaves from this line is to be avoided. We have to express a sense of tension resulting from a plant rising from the water line leisurely, but supporting the whole body at the water edge.

Combination

Shoka is arranged with simple structures and reveals the fresh beauty of plants. Shoka has simplified the complexity of Nature, and it has made a strong impression on Ikebana. Only one species is arranged when the branches have flowers attached. If the branches have no flowers, a kind of plant or grass with flowers is used in the Tai part. This is called "Nejime." Plant materials with a weaker force than the materials used for Shin and Soe are used as Nejime.

HOIKUSHA COLOR BOOKS

ENGLISH EDITIONS

Book Size 4″ × 6″

COLORED ILLUSTRATIONS FOR NATURALISTS

Text in Japanese, with index in Latin or English.

First Issues (Book Size 6″ × 8″)

1. BUTTERFLIES of JAPAN
2. INSECTS of JAPAN vol.1
3. INSECTS of JAPAN vol.2
4. SHELLS of JAPAN vol.1
5. FISHES of JAPAN vol.1
6. BIRDS of JAPAN
7. MAMMALS of JAPAN
8. SEA SHORE ANIMALS of JAPAN
9. GARDEN FLOWERS vol.1
10. GARDEN FLOWERS vol.2
11. ROSES and ORCHIDS
12. ALPINE FLORA of JAPAN vol.1
13. ROCKS
14. ECONOMIC MINERALS
15. HERBACEOUS PLANTS of JAPAN vol.1
16. HERBACEOUS PLANTS of JAPAN vol.2
17. HERBACEOUS PLANTS of JAPAN vol.3
18. SEAWEEDS of JAPAN
19. TREES and SHRUBS of JAPAN
20. EXOTIC AQUARIUM FISHES vol.1
21. MOTHS of JAPAN vol.1
22. MOTHS of JAPAN vol.2
23. FUNGI of JAPAN vol.1
24. PTERIDOPHYTA of JAPAN
25. SHELLS of JAPAN vol.2
26. FISHES of JAPAN vol.2
27. EXOTIC AQUARIUM FISHES vol.2
28. ALPINE FLORA of JAPAN vol.2
29. FRUITS
30. REPTILES and AMPHIBIANS of JAPAN
31. ECONOMIC MINERALS vol.2
32. FRESHWATER FISHES of JAPAN
33. GARDEN PLANTS of the WORLD vol.1
34. GARDEN PLANTS of the WORLD vol.2
35. GARDEN PLANTS of the WORLD vol.3
36. GARDEN PLANTS of the WORLD vol.4
37. GARDEN PLANTS of the WORLD vol.5
38. THE FRESHWATER PLANKTON of JAPAN
39. MEDICINAL PLANTS of JAPAN

SHELLS
OF
THE
WESTERN
PACIFIC
IN
COLOR

Book Size 7″×10″

⟨vol. I⟩ by Tetsuaki Kira
(304 pages, 72 in color)
⟨vol. II⟩ by Tadashige Habe
(304 pages, 66 in color)

FISHES
OF
JAPAN
IN
COLOR

Book Size 7″×10″

by Toshiji Kamohara
(210 pages, 64 in color)